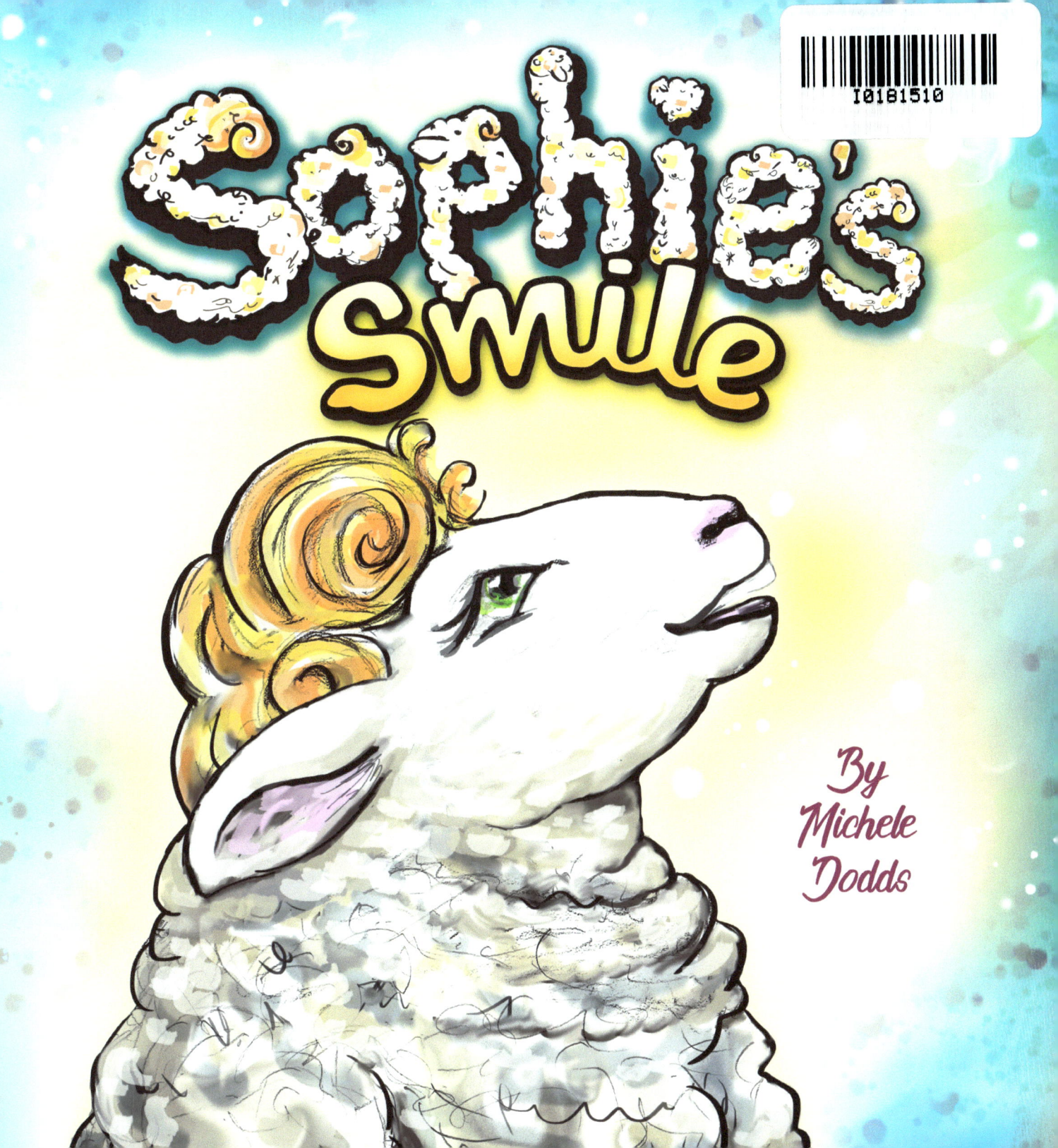

The Good Shepherd feeds his flock and gently leads those with their young. He carries them and keeps them close to his heart. Reference Isaiah 40:11.

Sophie's Smile
©2025 Text and Illustrations

All rights reserved. No portion of this book may be reproduced, stored in a retrieval system, or transmitted in any form or by any means - electronic, mechanical, photocopy, recording, scanning, or other - except for brief quotations in critical reviews or articles, without the prior written permission of the author.

Written and Illustrated by Michele Dodds
©2025   Dedicated to my mother.
ISBN: 978-1-965323-14-4

Smile!

Once upon a time there was a sheep named Sophie, whose smile was as bright as the orange curl on her head. Her arms waved in joy when the flock singing she led. One day a handsome ram blew in with the wind. He liked Sophie's smile. Before long they said, "I do."

Sophie invited lonely sheep over for tea. She asked them to smile too. Soon photos and memory books filled the house. Sophie felt happy and blessed, but Dadram felt crowded and stressed.

When Dadram was offered a job up north, he jumped up and said, "Quick, Sophie, grab what will fit!" And off we drove, lickety-split.

Upon arriving, Dadram found a place in Poverty Valley. He said,
"Sophie, where's your smile? Don't worry, we'll only be here a while.
Mel and Dew, stay out of the forest. Don't go under the overpass.
That busy highway is not for a lamb child.
And stay away from the lake where the wolves run wild."

Dadram left. Sophie's smile left too.
Poverty Valley became the Valley of Thorns, and we were stuck in the thicket.
As we stared out the window, I heard Sophie softly say,
"Dadram will come back to us one day."

Before long, Sophie heard the news. Dadram had a new family to feed. The burrs and thorns of heartbreak stuck Sophie deep. All she could do was weep.

Meanwhile, Mel and I tried to be helpful. At Lamb School, Mel did very well. At home she sewed stylish aprons to sell.

I found empty bottles in the forest and under the overpass.
I ran across the busy highway to trade them for cash.

One day I searched for bottles
near the forbidden lake.
A pack of wolves ran out of the forest and chased me.
One wolf scratched my leg. I needed a doctor,
but Sophie couldn't drive.

"Mommy, will I turn into a vicious beast and die from the wild wolf disease?" I cried.

But thankfully...

I survived.

Sometimes Dadram came to visit us.
He took Mel and me to the beach to play in the tides.
The waves tossed us to and fro.
Poor Sophie longed to be included
but never got to go.

Soon Sophie began to change. She thought less and less about Dadram. She almost smiled again.
Then one sunny morning, Sophie sat down and wrote a letter to a farmkeeper far away, asking about a new place where we could stay.

"Watch out!"

"RUN!"

With the money we had saved,
Sophie bought an old car.
She bravely clung to the steering wheel.
"Sheep really aren't meant to drive
you know!" She yelled
as the tires peeled. Lambs jumped.
One ram even squealed.

Finally, Sophie received a reply to her letter.
"They want us!" She bleated in shock.
We loaded a Ewe Hauler with help from the flock.
Mel and I waved goodbye, feeling free at last,
as Sophie sheepishly pressed her foot on the gas.

When we arrived that night, Sophie showed the letter to the farmkeeper.
He sadly said, "I'm sorry ma'am, you misunderstood; this is a hotel."
She ran back in such a panic, she almost fell.
"Poor Mommy!" We yelled.

Sophie pulled her wool together and parked on an abandoned road.
We crawled into the back and made a shelter amongst the load.
Sophie found the card the wise ram had given to her.
She read the words out loud to us:

TO Sophie,
The GOOD SHEPHERD himself will lead you and be with you. He will not fail you or abandon you. So do not lose courage or be afraid.
Deuteronomy 31:8

Years later, the Good Shepherd brought a sweet ram to the fold. He and Sophie married. Together they sang songs to praise the Good Shepherd, their whole lives long.

www.ingramcontent.com/pod-product-compliance
Lightning Source LLC
LaVergne TN
LVHW072058070426
835508LV00002B/163